Better Credit in 90 Days Or Less

First Edition

By Dewayne Gleeton

I dedicate this book to my loving family, and especially to my beautiful granddaughter Kylee. My best friend Kylee!

Dewayne Gleeton

Table of contents

Better Credit in 90 Days Or Less

This book comes with a software download that includes the following:

- **Credit Repair Letters**
  Credit repair letters for different situations that are optimized and written to help you get items removed from your credit.

- **Bankruptcy 101**
  This is a booklet that explains all about bankruptcy. It explains the different types, how they work and much more.

- **Fair Credit Reporting Act**
  We have included a complete copy of the fair credit reporting act so that you can see and use the law.

- **Budget Planning Software**
  Excel based software designed to help you keep and manage your monthly budget. It has all you need to manage, and control your budget so that you can save and invest more.

How To Make Extra Money Ebooks

A great collection of how to books that can show you step by step ways to make extra money. These books cover everything from garage sales to internet sales. This is worth hundreds of dollars in future profits for you!

After purchase send an email to: ceo.advantas@gmail.com **for the free download.**

Your Personal Credit Report

Let's face it; if you want a great credit report, then you must pay your bills on time. However, many credit reports have errors and old information that hurt your credit and should be removed via the credit repair process.

Each credit report contains five main areas of information. These areas are:

- Personal
    - Name
    - Current and previous address
    - Social security number
    - Telephone number
    - Date of birth
    - Employers
- Public Record information
    - Collections
    - Bankruptcies
    - Tax liens
    - Judgments

- Credit History
  - Bank loans
  - Retail credit
  - Loans & mortgages
  - Student loans
  - Credit
- Inquiries
- Summative Credit Score

Whit is my credit score and how do I get it?

Your summative credit score is a result of many factors. It is calculated and assigned to you by companies based on different factors. The four main factors in this equation are Credit, Cash flow, collateral and character.

Credit

The credit report plays a tremendous part in you obtaining the credit or things in life you want such as cars and homes. Most times in today's economy it is the only one of the four considered in making the loan decisions. By looking at your past payment history lenders can assume that a reflection of the other three factors is evident.

Cash flow

This is a vital part of your financial health and future. I write about it in my book on budgeting. To creditors, cash flow help to determine if the borrower can afford the payments. (The financial collapse of 2008 was due to creditors letting people borrow much more than their cash flow could reasonable be sustained when interest rates rose.) Cash flow rules say that your mortgage cannot exceed 28 percent of your monthly income and your total debt ratio cannot be more than 36 percent of your total monthly income.

Collateral

The ability to have collateral is not as important in credit decisions as it used to be. The only time it plays a factor is in the case of car and home loans, where the item being purchased is also collateral for the loan. The rule for collateral is the more you have the better you are.

Character

Creditors look for stability and honesty. They look at your history in relationship to your work, living and criminal records. Work history at a job is very important.

What is good and bad credit?

A good credit score is what each of us aspires to. After all, a credit score is one of the important determining factors when it comes to borrowing money – and getting a low rate when you do.

But trying to pin down a specific number that means your credit score is "good" can be tricky. When it comes to figuring out what makes a good credit score, there are a few different schools of thought.

Most credit scores – including the FICO score and the latest version of the Vantage Score – operate within the range of 301 to 850. Within that range, there are different categories, from bad to excellent.

- Excellent Credit: 781 – 850
- Good Credit: 661-780
- Fair Credit: 601-660
- Poor Credit: 501-600
- Bad Credit: below 500

But even these aren't set in stone. That's because lenders all have their own definitions of what is a good credit score. One lender that is looking to approve more borrowers might approve applicants with credit scores of 680 or higher. Another might be more selective and only approve those with scores of 750 or higher. Or both lenders might offer credit to anyone with a score of at least 650, but charge consumers with scores below 700 a higher interest rate!

There are many different credit scores available to lenders, and they each develop their own credit score range. Why is that important? Because if you get your credit score, you need to know the credit score range you are looking at so you understand where your number fits in.

The Credit Score Range Using Various Scoring Models:

- FICO Score range: 300-850
- Vantage Score 3.0 range: 300–850
- Vantage Score scale (versions 1.0 and 2.0): 501–990
- PLUS Score: 330-830
- Trans Risk Score: 100-900
- Equifax Credit Score: 280–850

With all of the scores listed above, the higher the number the lower the risk. That means consumers with higher scores are more likely to get approved for credit, and to get the best interest rates when they do. And they are more likely to get discounts on insurance. What is considered a "high" score depends on what type of score is being used.

If you have a FICO score of 840, for example, you're just 10 points shy of the highest score possible and your credit is "super prime." But if you have an 840 Vantage Score (using version 2.0), it's not as spectacular because you're 150 points away from the highest possible score.

What's Your Score?

Don't assume your score is good (or isn't) just because you have always paid your bills on time (or haven't.) The only way to know whether you have a good credit score is to check.

What Can I Get With A Good Credit Score?

Some of the best credit cards–from rewards cards to 0% balance transfer offers–go to consumers with strong credit scores. A good credit score can also get you a lower interest rate when you borrow. That means you will pay less over time. For example, if you're buying a $300,000 house with a 30 year fixed mortgage, and you have good credit, then you could end up paying more than $90,000 less for that house over the life of the loan than if you had bad credit.

 What are side effects of bad credit?

"What's the big deal with a low credit score," you might ask. Since so many businesses now judge you based on your credit score, having bad credit can make life extremely difficult from getting a job to getting a place to live. Here are some of the most common side-effects of bad credit.

1. High interest rates on your credit cards and loans

Creditors and lenders see bad credit applicants as riskier than applicants with better credit scores. They make you pay for this risk by giving you a higher interest rate. Over time you'll end up paying more in interest than you would if you have better credit and a better interest rate. The cost is higher with big credit card balances or major loans.

2. Credit and loan applications may not be approved

Because creditors and lenders think your bad credit is a risk, they might not want to lend to you at all. You may find that your applications are being denied.

3. Difficulty getting approved for an apartment

Who knew that landlords checked credit before allowing you to sign a lease? It's true. Having bad credit can leave you homeless or close to it.

4. Security deposits on utilities

Utility companies – electricity, phone, and cable – check your credit as part of the application process. If you have a bad credit history, you may have to pay a security deposit to establish service in your name, even if you've always paid your utility bills on time.

5. You can't get a cell phone contract

Yep, cell phone companies check your credit too. They contend that they're extending a month of service to you, so they need to know how reliable your payments will be. If your credit's bad, you may have to get a prepaid cell phone, a month-to-month contract where phones are typically more expensive, or go without one at all.

6. You might get denied for employment

Certain jobs, especially those in upper management or the finance industry, require you to have a good credit history. You can actually be turned down for a job because of negative items on your credit report, especially high debt amounts, bankruptcy, or outstanding bills.

7. Higher insurance premiums

Insurance companies check credit too. They say that lower credit scores are linked to higher claims filed. Because of this theory, they check your credit and charge a higher premium to those with lower credit scores, regardless of the number of claims you've actually filed.

8. Calls from debt collectors

Bad credit itself doesn't lead to debt collection calls. However, chances are if you have bad credit you also have some past due bills that debt collectors are pursuing.

9. Difficulty starting your own business

Many new businesses need banks loans to help fund their startup. A bad credit history can limit the amount you're able to borrow to start a new business, even if you have the greatest idea and the data to prove it.

10. Difficulty purchasing a car

Banks check your credit before giving you a car loan. With bad credit you might get denied or you might get approved with a high interest rate. Most of those "no credit check" and "we finance" car lots charge extremely high interest rates that make it difficult to make your monthly car payments.

11. Get a Promotion

Employers check credit before deciding to hire you. Some government, financial, management, and executive jobs are particularly curious about your financial history. A bad credit history could cost you the job, or the promotion you've been working hard to get.

12. Take some financial pressure off your spouse

When one spouse has better credit than the other, the spouse with good credit will be the one applying for the loans and credit cards. Improving your credit will let you bear some of the credit-brunt rather than placing it entirely on your spouse.

13. Stop relying on co-signers

When you have bad credit, you'll often need others to co-sign for your loans and credit cards. If you can find someone to co-sign, you're putting financial pressure on them but they don't receive any of the benefit. Repairing your credit will save you the time and hassle of burdening someone else with being a co-signer.

14. Start your own business

Starting a new business takes money; so many entrepreneurs rely on small business loans to get their businesses of the ground. Bad credit can keep you from getting the financing you need to start your new business. You'll have to improve your credit before a bank will give you a loan.

15. Protect your children's credit score

Having bad credit can tempt you to use your child's credit. You might think you'd never do that but you never know what you'll do when you're desperate. Say you have to have electricity turned on, but your credits too bad. You could easily rationalize using your child's credit to have the electricity turned on. Keep your own good credit and you won't think about exploiting your child's.

How do I keep a good credit score?

In this book we are going to show you how to fix your credit. It is important to know the information in this section before and after fixing your credit. Once we have fixed it, it is up to you to continue to build and maintain a high credit score by using these reminders.

1. Know what goes into a good credit score.

The more you know about what goes into your credit score, the better. Also, it will be easier it will be to maintain a good one. Five key pieces of information are used to calculate your credit score – your payment history, level of debt, credit age, mix of credit, and recent credit. But, not everything financial affects your credit score. For example, checking account overdrafts and utility payments won't automatically help (or hurt) your credit score. Our credit score is a three-digit number that is used to predict how you will pay your bills. The score ranges from 300-850 and is calculated using your credit history information from your credit report. When you make an application for credit, the creditor or lender uses your credit score to quickly make a credit/no-credit decision. This same decision can very well be made by simply viewing your credit report, but the credit score makes decision-making easier and less subjective.

While there are several different versions of the credit score, the most commonly used version is the FICO score (Read FICO vs. FAKO). Developed by the Fair Isaac Company, the FICO score is used by many creditors and lenders to decide whether or not to extend credit to you.

How To Calculate A Credit Score

Because some parts of your bill-paying history are more important than others, different pieces of your credit history are given different weights in calculating your credit score. Even though the specific equation for coming up with your credit score is proprietary information owned by Fair Isaac, we do know what information is used to calculate your score.

Payment history is 35%

Lenders are most concerned about whether or not you pay your bills. The best indicator of this is how you've paid your bills in the past. Late payments, collections, and bankruptcies all affect the payment history of your credit score. More recent delinquencies hurt your credit score more than those in the past.

Debt level is 30%

The amount of debt you have in comparison to your credit limits is known as credit utilization. The higher your credit utilization – the closer you are to your limits – the lower your credit score will be. Keep your credit card balances at about 30% of your credit limit or less.

Length of credit history 15%

Having a longer credit history is favorable because it gives more information about your spending habits. It's good to leave open the accounts that you've had for a long time.

Inquiries are 10%

Each time you make an application for credit, an inquiry is added to your credit report. Too many applications for credit can mean that you are taking on a lot of debt or that you are in some kind of financial trouble. While inquiries can remain on your credit report for two years, your credit score calculation only considers those made within a year.

Mix of credit is 10%

Having different kinds of accounts is favorable because it shows that you have experience managing a mix of credit. This isn't a significant factor in your credit score unless you don't have much other information on which to base your score. Open new accounts as you need them, not to simply have what seems like a better mix of credit.

2. Pay your bills on time.

That goes for all your bills, not just your credit cards and loans. While certain bills don't get reported to the credit bureaus when you pay on time, they could end up on your credit report if you fall behind. Even a small library fine could wind up on your credit report if it's left unpaid. Continue to pay all your bills on time to maintain a good credit score.

3. Keep your credit card balances low.

The higher your credit card balance is, the worse your credit score will be. ***Your credit card balance should be within 30% of your credit limit to maintain a good credit score***. That's $300 on a credit card with a $1,000 credit limit. Charging more than 30% of your credit limit is risky even if you plan to pay off the balance when your billing statement comes. Card issuers typically report the balance when your statement closes and if that's a high balance; your credit score will be affected even if you subsequently pay your balance in full.

If you do this with all of your credit cards, it's possible to lose 30% of your credit score in this area!

4. Manage your debt.

Credit card balances aren't the only accounts that influence your credit score. Loan balances and lines of credit also impact your level of debt (30% of your credit score). Having too much debt can cost credit score points and make it difficult to afford your monthly payments. The lower your debt, the easier it will be to maintain a good credit score.

5. Don't close old credit cards.

When you close a credit card, your credit card issuer no longer sends updates to the credit bureaus and the credit scoring formula places less weight on inactive accounts. After 10 years or so, the credit bureau will remove that closed account's history from your credit report. If the account was an old one (which it would be after 10+ years), losing that credit history will shorten your average credit age and cause your credit score to drop. Here are five credit cards that you should never close and why it's better to leave them open.

1. Don't close any credit card that still has a balance.

When you close a credit card with a balance, your total available credit and credit limit are reported as $0. Since you still have a balance on that credit card with no credit limit, it looks like you've maxed out. A maxed out credit card, or one that appears to be maxed out, can have a very negative impact on your credit score since your level of credit card debt, including your credit usage to available credit ratio, is 30% of your credit score.

2. Don't close your only credit card with available credit.

Closing out this card will decrease total available credit and, subsequently, increase your total credit utilization. Just like closing a credit card with a balance, closing one without a balance can also affect your credit score, because you've used up all the credit that's available to you.

3. Don't close your only credit card.

Since part of your credit score (10%) is based on the different types of credit you have, keeping a credit card in the mix will add points to our credit score. Leave your only credit card open to show that you have experience managing various types of credit accounts.

4. Don't close your oldest credit card account.

Closing out old credit cards shortens your credit history. Lenders tend to view borrowers with short credit histories as riskier than borrowers with longer histories. Closing your oldest credit card won't impact your credit score immediately. But, once the credit card falls off your credit report several years down the road, you might see an unexpected credit score drop.

5. Don't close the credit card with the best terms.

Why let a good thing go? If you have a credit card with a low interest rate, no annual fee, and other perks like travel insurance or great rewards, keep it. A credit card that charges you less for making purchases is far better than one that charges you more.

When to Close a Credit Card

It's ok to close a newer credit card that you no longer use as long as the card doesn't have a balance and you have other credit cards. Also, you might close a credit card that suddenly raises your interest rate or introduces an annual fee. Your credit card issuer will probably close the credit card for you if you decide to reject these new credit card terms. Finally, in identity theft and fraud situations, your creditors will advise you to close the credit card to keep the thief from damaging your credit even further.

Close Your Credit Card the Right Way

Always close a credit card by sending a written notice to the card issuer. You can call first to cancel your account, but always follow up with a letter confirming your desire to have the credit card closed. Follow up by making sure the credit card is reported as "Closed" on your credit report. It won't necessarily hurt your credit score if the credit card continues to be reported "Open," but double checking will ensure your card is indeed closed. You should be just as selective about the credit cards you close as the ones you open. Before you pick up the phone to alert your creditor that you want to close your account, make sure it's not going to affect your credit score in a negative way.

6. Limit your applications for new credit.

Each time you apply for credit – whether a credit card or loan – your credit score takes a small hit. Credit inquiries are only 10% of your credit scores, but if you have a high credit score (say 800), you stand to lose a lot of points (10% of 800 is 80). Opening a new credit account also lowers your average credit age (15% of your credit score). To maintain a good credit score, you should open new credit sparingly.

7. Watch your credit report.

Just because you do everything right with your credit doesn't mean everyone else will. Errors could end up on your credit report leading to a drop in your credit score. Identity theft and credit card fraud can also lead to inaccurate information on your credit report. Checking your credit report throughout the year lets you detect these mistakes sooner so you can correct them and maintain a good credit score.

Federal law - the Fair and Accurate Credit Transactions Act of 2003 - gives you the right to a free credit report every year from each of the three credit bureaus - Equifax, Experian, and TransUnion. This is your annual credit report. There are a lot of impostor websites on the internet promising to give your free annual credit report. These sites typically request your credit card information and enroll you in a trial membership to a credit monitoring service. If you don't cancel the trial, your credit card will end up getting charged for a full period of the credit monitoring service.

The true website for ordering your annual credit report doesn't require a credit card and doesn't ask you to sign up for any trial subscription.

3 Ways to Order Your Annual Credit Report

To order your annual credit report online, visit www.annualcreditreport.com. If you are suspicious about a link to the legitimate annual credit report website, you can type the address directly into your web browser making sure not to misspell the address. You can also order your annual credit report over the phone by calling 1-877-322-8228. If you choose this option, there will be a verification process to ensure you (and not someone else) are actually ordering your credit report. If you are deaf or hard of hearing, you can call 1-800-821-7232 to order your annual credit report.

Finally, you can order your annual credit report via mail. To do this, you should first download and print an annual credit report request form. The form requires an Adobe viewer. Once you have completed the form, you can mail it to:

Annual Credit Report Request Service

P.O. Box 105281

Atlanta, GA 30348-5281

When you order by phone or mail, you will receive your annual credit report via mail within 2 to 3 weeks. You must order your annual credit report using one of the methods listed above. You cannot receive your government-granted annual credit report directly from the credit bureaus. Note that all the credit bureaus have a free credit report offer, but these offers require a credit card and you may not be able to order another free credit report next year.

You can order all three annual credit reports at one time or you can space them out over the year. For example, you might order your Equifax annual credit report in April, Experian in August, Trans-Union in December, and start over with Equifax the next April. This allows you to monitor your credit reports throughout the entire year.

Annual Credit Score – How to get a free look at your scores

The annual credit report does not include a credit score, free or paid. You can order your credit score from myFICO.com or one of the three credit bureaus.

You can get a free credit score look by signing up at www.creditkarma.com. This is a great site to use, (no credit card needed) to monitor your credit score as you try to fix and improve your credit score.

Order Your Credit Report

Equifax 1-800-685-1111 - you can get a free report if you have been denied credit in the last 60 days. Make sure that you order only the credit report. Mail within 48 hours.

Trans-Union 1-800-888-4213 - receive within 6 to 8 business days.

Experian 1-888-397-3742 - receive within 8 to 10 business days.

Caution: If your phone request gets lost, you'll have to write to them anyway. If your letter is after 30 days of being denied credit, employment, or insurance, you might have to pay for the report. It would be a good idea to mention in your letter the date that you requested the report by phone. Your written request should contain proof of your identity and current address, such as your driver's license and a copy of a utility bill.

Mailing Addresses for Credit Bureaus

Experian

P.O. Box 4500

Allen, TX 75013

Equifax Credit Information Services, Inc.

P.O. Box 740256

Atlanta, GA 30348

Trans-Union, LLC

P.O. Box 2000

Chester, PA 19022

Information Needed When Requesting a Credit Report

When requesting a credit report or writing a letter to the credit bureaus disputing a negative item, it is a good idea to include all of the below information.

The more information you provide to them at the beginning, the less likely you will get a letter back from them requesting additional verification - that only prolongs the process. Remember to always make copies of what you mail to the bureaus for your records and always remember to sign your request. You should provide:

- Your Full Legal Name

- Your Date of Birth
- Social Security Number
- Current Mailing Address
- If Less Than 5 Years, Include Your Previous Address
- A Copy of Your Driver's License Showing Your Current Address
- A Copy of Your Social Security Card - If Your SS Number Is Not On Your Driver's License

If you have a letter denying you credit, employment, or insurance within the last 30 days, a copy of the letter should be provided, since this will allow you to obtain a free copy of your credit report.

If you ordered your credit report, within 10 to 30 days you should receive a copy of your credit report from each of the agencies.

If you are disputing items on your reports, the credit bureaus are required to respond in writing within 30 days of receipt of your letter.

Note: *It's always a good idea to send your correspondence via registered mail so you have proof the credit bureau received your request during disputes.*

Can I really fix my credit?

Of course you can! Many of our readers and even yours truly have cleared up a few blemishes on their reports. And by the way: **everything a credit repair clinic can do for you, you can do for yourself at little or no cost.**

What the information provided in this book does is help you fix **ERRORS** on your credit report and clean up those "questionable" items. While no one can legally remove accurate negative information from a credit report, the law does allow you to request a reinvestigation of information in your file that you dispute as inaccurate or incomplete. However, it is perfectly legal to challenge ANYTHING on your credit report. If there were or are **ERRORS**, It has to be removed. *There is no charge for requesting an investigation.*

The whole key to the credit repair procedure is that if the credit bureaus cannot verify information on your credit report they must remove it.

For instance, if a credit bureau cannot contact a collection agency, which is reporting a collection on your report, they cannot verify the information, and the credit bureau must delete the entry.

Basic Credit Repair Strategy

The basic strategy to repairing your credit is as follows:

1. Get and review your credit report.
2. Analyze your report.
3. Make a list of all items you consider to be questionable or negative. Clearly identify each item in your report that you dispute, explain why you dispute the information,
4. Write a dispute letter to the bureau.
5. Send the letter to the credit bureaus. Make sure you send it registered or certified mail.
6. Document your efforts. Record when you sent your letters, and the results.
7. Wait for the bureaus to investigate your claims.
8. Analyze the results.
9. Specialized techniques Was the item deleted or changed to your satisfaction? You may continue steps 1, 2 and 3 above until you feel the dispute is settled satisfactorily. Remember, there is no charge for a reinvestigation. If you don't get the results you want, dispute the listing again.

That's all there is to it. Seems easy enough but you must have patience, because the credit bureaus are not always very cooperative. They make their money by providing credit reports to lenders not by fixing bad information in their databases.

Analyzing your credit report

When you first receive your Trans Union and Equifax credit reports, you will be totally lost. The average consumer codes the information in a way that is not immediately readable.

 Each credit report should arrive with a key that interprets the codes and indicators on the credit report. Sit down with the credit report and the key and study it until you understand what each number and code means.

Important: Don't write on your original credit report yet. Make all of your notes on a copy of the report. You will be sending your original report with your dispute letter, so you should make at least two copies of each new report. *The original goes with the dispute, one copy is for notes, and the other copy is what you will send in to the credit agency*.

Gather a yellow and pink highlighter pen. Whenever you see a negative listing, mark the listing in yellow on your scratch copy of the credit report.

Very often, it is difficult to tell if an item on the credit report is negative or positive.

The following table will help you identify every negative listing on your credit reports.

Negative Credit Indicators

If the listing contains one or more of these indicators, then the listing is negative. If the listing contains none of these indicators, then the listing is positive.

Experian (formerly TRW) Credit Report

- **Any item marked with an asterisk in any inquiry**

Trans Union Credit Report

- Any item rated higher than I1, M1, or R1.
- Any item listed as repossession, foreclosure, profit and loss write-off charge-off,
- Paid profit and loss
- Write-off, paid charge off, settled, settled for less than full balance, or included in bankruptcy
- Any collection amount, whether paid or not.
- Any court account, including a lien, judgment, bankruptcy chapters 11, 7, or 13, divorce, satisfied lien, or satisfied judgment.
- Any item showing one or more thirty, sixty, or ninety-day late payments in the column to the far right.
- Any inquiry.

Equifax Credit Report

- Any item rated higher than I1, M1, or R1 (such as R2 or I9).
- Any item proceeded by a ">>>>" icon.
- Any item listed as repossession, foreclosure, profit and loss write-off charge-off, paid profit and loss write-off, paid charge off, settled, settled for less than full balance, or included in bankruptcy.
- Any collection amount, whether paid or not.
- Any court account, including a lien, judgment, bankruptcy chapters 11, 7, or 13, divorce, satisfied lien, or satisfied judgment.
- Any item showing one or more thirty, sixty, or ninety-day late payments in the column to the far right.
- Any inquiry.

Those I2 and R9 codes - what do they mean?

R- Revolving (usually a credit card)
I - installment (like home or auto loan)

R1 or I1 = pays as agreed never late
R2 or I2 = 30 days late
R3 or I3 = 60 days late
R4 or I4 = 90 days late
R5 or I5 = 120 days late
R7 or I7 = making regular payments under wage earner plan
R8 or I8 = repossession
R9 or I9 = charge off

Generic FICO Scores

It's more common nowadays to use a shared scoring system. The "branded" name is FICO and it's quickly becoming the "generic" term (much like Band-Aid and Q-Tip respectively). This scoring system allows lenders to see your "big picture" without needing to look line by line to see if you've been naughty or nice.

Some lenders will have automatic disqualifiers such as Bankruptcies, Charge off's or simply from being late in the last 6 months etc. regardless of your score.

What it means:

O = Open (entire amount due each month i.e. AMEX)

R = Revolving (payment amount variable i.e. VISA)

I = Installment (fixed number of payments i.e. Auto loans)

0 = Approved, no rating

1 = Paid as agreed

2 = 30+ days late

3 = 60+ days late

4 = 90+ days late

5 = 120+ days late or collection

7 = Making regular payments under wage earner or similar plan

8 = Repossession

9 = Charged off to bad debt

J = Joint

I = Individual

U = Undesignated

A = Authorized User

T = Terminated

M = Maker

C = Co-Maker/Co-Signer

B = On behalf of another person

S = Shared

This is all the information you will need to repair your credit and begin to pay less for the money you borrow.

Roll up your sleeves and get started!

1. Get your credit report. (From all 3 major credit bureaus)

2. Analyze your credit report.

3. Rank questionable/negative items

Step 2 covered how to identify items, both positive and negative on your credit report. Now you have this list, you should rank each item according to the amount of damage they are doing to your overall credit picture. Rank the most damaging information first, followed by the next most damaging information, followed by those items, which are neutral.

Do this for each credit report, as remember, they may not all have the same information on them.

They may even have duplicate information. If this is the case, you will need to write to each credit agency individually for each duplicate item.

Items That Hurt Your Credit

The items here are listed in order of descending importance with the first item being the "most damaging" to your credit.

- Bankruptcy
- Foreclosure
- Repossession
- Loan Default
- Court Judgments
- Collections
- Past due payments
- Late Payments
- Credit Rejections
- Credit Inquiries

Also, if your creditor has NOT notified you of negative information they have recently placed on your credit report, they are currently in violation of the Fair Credit Reporting Act. *You can use this to pressure the original creditor to remove the listing by reminding them they are in violation of the FCRA by not notifying you.*

Requesting Corrections

What should you challenge? Challenge everything!

You should always shoot for a complete deletion. Don't bother challenging **the information within** a collection listing, charge-off, court record, repossession, foreclosure, or settled account. As the basic nature of these listings is negative, changing the information within the listing will yield no improvement. **Severely negative listings, such as these, must be disputed on the basis of complete deletion or not be disputed at all.**

What items are the toughest to get off your report?

You will have the toughest time getting bankruptcies and foreclosures off of your credit report as these things are so easy for the credit bureaus to verify. In the case of a bankruptcy, you most likely will have a few trade lines saying "included in Bankruptcy".

If you want to challenge your bankruptcy, you need to clear off all credit lines mentioning a BK FIRST.

Make sure you send everything registered or certified mail.

This is important, as you must be able to tell when letters were sent and received. It gives you some leverage with the Agencies if they don't respond in the time frame required by law.

Document Your Credit Repair Efforts

You Must Create A Precise Organizational System To Track Your Correspondences

As soon as you have ordered your credit reports and photocopied your order letters and checks, you must create a precise organizational system to track your correspondences with the credit bureaus and your creditors. Why is this necessary? Unfortunately, credit items you have worked so hard to remove mysteriously reappear. *If this happens, it is usually easy to have the items deleted permanently if you show your complete records on the first removal.* Why take a chance? As you proceed through these steps, keep copies and records of all correspondence you send and receive. **Copies of all correspondence are a must, as well as notes on all telephone conversations!**

If using a cell phone, there are several apps that will record your cell phone conversation for you. A very good one is called "call recorder"

Also, if you should encounter any special difficulty and would like help in repairing your credit, you will need these records to proceed. Every time you have a telephone conversation with a creditor, you must document the conversation by recording the name of the person to whom you spoke, his or her position, the date and time of the conversation, what was said in the conversation, and what was agreed upon.

Wait for the credit bureau to finishing investigating

Once the credit reporting agency has received your dispute letter, they are obligated to investigate. This obligation is not contingent upon you having been denied credit. According to the Fair Credit Reporting Act of 1997, the credit bureaus must take the following steps:

- The credit reporting agencies must resolve consumers' disputes within 30 days limit
- **In response to consumers' complaints that documentation in support of their disputes was disregarded, the credit bureaus have to consider and transmit to the furnisher all relevant evidence submitted by the consumer the first time.**
- Consumers will receive written notice of the results of the investigation within five days of its completion, including a copy of the amended credit file if it changed based on the dispute.
- Once information is deleted from a credit file, the credit bureaus cannot reinsert it unless the entity supplying the information certifies that the item is complete and accurate and the credit bureau notifies the consumer within **five** days.

The Federal Trade Commission says that inaccurate credit reports are the number-one source of consumer complaints, and that it is quite common for problems to take six or more months to be resolved. All of the big-three agencies are working on making sure that all disputes are handled within 30 days.

If the new investigation reveals an error, you may ask that a corrected version of the report be sent to anyone who received your report within the past six months. *Job applicants can have corrected reports sent to anyone who received a report for employment purposes during the past two years.* However, this is unlikely to repair any damage done when your credit report was first pulled, so don't waste your time or energy on this approach.

Evaluate the results of your repair efforts.

You did save the original credit report your ordered, didn't you? And each item you challenged?

Good, you will need them to evaluate how well you did. It's all part of Step 5 above, documenting your efforts.

When you get your "repaired" credit report back from the credit bureaus, they will summarize what changed on your credit report due to your challenges. You can compare this list to your own notes or just to the previous credit report.

Specialized techniques:

Depending on the type of listing, you may also want to try these separate techniques:

- Collections - you should always try to use the *debt validation technique* on collections. This should be in addition to your credit repair efforts with the credit bureaus.

- Charge-offs. Try disputing the information *within the listing*, like the date the account was opened, the high balance, the amount owed, etc. If any of the information is incorrect, you have a good chance of getting the whole thing deleted off of your report.

- Judgments. If you were never served for a judgment, you may have a chance of getting it vacated (voided), or there may be other technicalities that you can use. Check out our new section on how to do this

The results of each item will have been resolved in one of five different ways:

1. If the listing is not mentioned in the results list, you must have forgotten to include it, or your request was not sufficiently clear. You will need to dispute the item again in your next dispute letter. The bureaus are legally obligated to respond in writing within 30 days, so if they don't, it is highly unlike they are ignoring you.

2. The disputed item was investigated but verified. If you don't get the item removed, most likely, the credit

bureaus will have just given you a cryptic reason as to why like "item verified." The creditor may have responded to the credit bureau's request for re-verification. They may have simply said that the listing was correct, and in this case, the bureau will take their word for it. Now it is up to you to prove to the bureau that the item is not correct. The law required that the bureaus accept any proof you may submit, as well as to pass any documentation you provide on to your creditor for consideration, so be sure to **send any documentation you can, if you didn't do it the** first time. You could also try disputing the listing again at a future time. Who knows, you may get lucky, and a different employee of the creditor may not be able to verify the item.

3. The disputed listing was investigated as to the correctness of the information within the listing (such as late pay notations) and the listing was found to be inaccurate or unverifiable. Remember, if the creditor doesn't respond to the bureau at all, this is the same as the listing being unverifiable. In this case, the negative listing will now show up as a positive listing, or it will be deleted from your report all together. This is the best possible outcome.

If you are not getting the desired results from the credit bureaus Credit bureau disputes are not handled by computers, but by people, so the possibility that your claims was misunderstood, overlooked or mishandled is good. Fixing your credit takes time, and there is nothing you can do to expedite the process. **However, you can always resubmit your claims.**

Debt validation technique -The Right to Validate Your Debt

Under the FDCPA, you are allowed to validate this debt, and the creditor (in this case, the collection agency) must show provide your with one of the debt validation items listed above.

The specific section of the FDCPA:

FDCPA Section 809. Validation of debts [15 USC 1692g]

(b) If the consumer notifies the debt collector in writing within the thirty-day period described in subsection (a) that the debt, or any portion thereof, is disputed, or that the consumer requests the name and address of the original creditor, the debt collector shall cease collection of the debt, or any disputed portion thereof, until the debt collector obtains verification of the debt or any copy of a judgment, or the name and address of the original creditor, and a copy of such verification or judgment, or name and address of the original creditor, is mailed to the consumer by the debt collector.

The requirements for meeting debt validation are not tough. *However, it's not enough to send you a computer-generated printout of the debt.*

If a creditor can't validate a debt:

- They are not allowed to collect the debt,
- They are not allowed to contact you about the debt, and

They are also not allowed to report it under the Fair Credit Reporting Act (FCRA). Doing so is a violation of the FCRA, and the FCRA states that you can sue for $1,000 in damages for any violation of the Act.

A collection agency CANNOT report a debt to the credit bureaus which has not been validated, and, you can sue in federal or state court if you have them on a violation. You could receive $1,000 for the incident plus damages.

Small claims court, anyone? What to do if a collection agency responds to your request for validation with a summons to appear.

I've heard that some collection agencies are starting to respond to validation requests with summons to appear in court. There is precedent which says that a collection agency cannot even file suit against you if they haven't validated the debt within the initial 30 day period.

If this happens to you, you may cite the case: Spears vs. Brennan

The appeals court determined:

"Brennan (plaintiff collection agency attorney) violated 15 U.S.C. § 1692g(b) when he obtained a default judgment against Spears (defendant) after Spears had notified Brennan in writing that the debt was being disputed and before Brennan had mailed verification of the debt to Spears."

This means that you have an absolute defense in court to deny them judgment if they still have not validated the debt. Once you get your FDCPA dispute letter in, the collector cannot even get a judgment until they satisfy the FDCPA law. The appeals court overturned the default summary judgment in part because the collection agency lawyer did not meet the rules of the FDCPA.

This could be grounds for getting a default judgment vacated. It's also another violation of the FDCPA and you can collect $1,000 from them.

The Debt Validation Strategy

Dispute the collection with the credit bureaus.

Look up the Statute of Limitations (SOL) on the debt. If the debt is past the statute of limitations, send them a letter informing that they are trying to collect zombie debt. This is debt which is too old to have any legal liability for a consumer.

If the collection agency does not remove the listing after you point out the SOL, sometimes your only remedy is to sue them.

If the debt is not past the statute of limitations, send a letter requesting validation to the collection agency

Wait 30 days to hear back from the collection agency. Most likely they will not respond or they will respond saying that they received your letter. Only a letter which includes one of the following:

- Proof that the collection company owns the debt/or has been assigned the debt.
- Copies of statements from the original creditor.
- Copy of the original signed loan agreement or credit card application.
- Copy of a cancelled check from you to the original creditor.

If they haven't sent you satisfactory proof, and are still reporting this on your report, *send a copy of your receipt for your registered mail, a copy of the first letter you sent and a statement that they have not complied with the FDCPA and are now in violation of the Act.*

Tell them they need to immediately remove the collection listing from your credit report or you are going to file a lawsuit because they are in violation of the FDCPA, section 809 (b).

Wait 15-20 days to hear back after this second letter to the collection agency. They will either remove it or not respond.

If they do provide a contract with a signature from the original creditor showing that you owe the debt, there is one more thing you can try: see if they are legally licensed to collect the debt in your state. Not all states require licensing.

If you believe that they are not licensed, and licensing is required in your state, write them another letter and tell them they are in violation of your state's collection laws and are subject to prosecution and fines. Cite your state's fines and procedures in the letter. This is a last ditch effort, but has worked in some cases.

Typically, your work will stop here, as most collection agencies will bow down to your demands and send you a letter agreeing to remove the listing. Now all you have to do is send a copy of the letter to the CRAs.

If the collection agency did not agree to remove the listing, then you need to continue to the next steps.

File a lawsuit in small claims court against the collection agency on the basis of violating the FDCPA.

Have the papers served to the collection agency. (You can find a paper server on the internet for about $25).

Also, in a parallel effort with your debt suit against the collection agency.

If the collection comes back as "verified" from the credit bureaus, you now have proof of further collection activity from the collection agency. (The assumption is that the credit bureau contacted the collection agency to verify the debt.) Since the collection agency did not validate the debt, further collection activity is a violation of the FDCPA.

Contact the credit bureaus, and tell them that the creditors did not verify the debts under the FDCPA, and send copies of your proof. Request the method of verification, which is your right under the FCRA. It is crucial to contact the credit bureaus before filing a lawsuit. Make sure you state that the collection agency did not respond to your request for debt validation.

You can try sending them this letter to see if they will budge. They may tell you that the request needs to come from the creditor. This is not true. If they can't give you reasonable information on how they verified the information and the collection agency has provided you none, you can conclude there was no reasonable investigation performed. They are teetering on the edge of "willful non-compliance" under the FCRA. Tell them so.

File a suit in small claims, state or federal court. The basis of the lawsuit should be that the credit bureaus could not provide a satisfactory method of verification, or did not conduct a reasonable investigation.

Have the papers served. Notify the bureaus that you are suing them. The credit bureaus will call the creditors and find out that there is a question about whether the debt is legitimate. They should delete it immediately.

Credit Freezes

Credit freezes, also known as security freezes, place a lock on access to a borrower's credit report. With a credit freeze in place, lenders and other companies cannot view the borrower's credit. As a result, freezes prevent the consumer from gaining access to new loans, such as credit cards and mortgages, but they also keep fraudsters from opening new accounts in that person's name. These freezes can subsequently be lifted temporarily or permanently by consumers, sometimes also for a price. However, in many states, you can avoid paying any fees at all by providing proof -- a police report, for example -- that you've already been a victim of fraud.

For anyone who is extremely concerned about the prospect of identity theft, there is no better tool than a credit freeze.

HOW TO "FREEZE" YOUR CREDIT FILES

If you live in California, you have the right to put a "security freeze" on your credit file. A security freeze means that your file cannot be shared with potential creditors. A security freeze can help prevent identity theft. Most businesses will not open credit accounts without first checking a consumer's credit history. If your credit files are frozen, even someone who has your name and Social Security number would probably not be able to get credit in your name.

A security freeze is free to identity theft victims who have a police report of identity theft. If you are not an identity theft victim and you are under 65 years of age, it will cost you $10 to place a freeze with each of the three credit bureaus. That is a total of $30 to freeze your files. If you are not an identity theft victim and you are 65 years of age or older, it will cost you $5 to place a freeze with each of the three credit bureaus. That is a total of $15 to freeze your files.

How do I place a security freeze?

To place a freeze, you must contact each of the three credit bureaus. You can request the freeze by mail. See the sample letters at the end of this sheet for addresses and what information to include. You may also place the freeze online. Here are the freeze web pages for the credit bureaus. Note: If these links do not work, search "security freeze" on the credit bureau web sites.

https://www.freeze.equifax.com

https://www.experian.com/freeze/center.html

http://www.transunion.com/personal-credit/credit-disputes/credit-freezes.page

If you are an identity theft victim, provide a copy of your police report (or DMV investigative report) of identity theft. Otherwise, if you are under 65 years of age, provide payment of $10 to each of the credit bureaus; if you are 65 years of age or older, provide payment of $5 to each of the credit bureaus.

Can I open new credit accounts if my files are frozen?

Yes. If you want to open a new credit account or get a new loan, you can lift the freeze on your credit file. You can lift it for a period of time. Or you can lift it for a specific creditor. After you contact the credit bureaus asking for the freeze, each credit bureau will send you a Personal Identification Number (PIN). You will also get instructions on how to lift the freeze by using your PIN. The credit bureaus must lift your freeze within three days.

For consumers under 65 years of age, the fee for lifting the freeze temporarily is $10 for a date-range lift or for a lift for a specific creditor. For consumers 65 years of age or older, the fee for either type of temporary lift is $5.

What is the difference between a fraud alert and a freeze?

A fraud alert is a special message on the report that a credit issuer receives when checking a consumer's credit rating. It tells the credit issuer that there may be fraud involved in the account. A fraud alert can help protect you against identity theft. A fraud alert can also slow down your ability to get new credit. It should not stop you from using your existing credit cards or other accounts. A security freeze means that your credit file cannot be seen by potential creditors, insurance companies, or employers doing background checks – unless you give your consent. Most businesses will not open credit accounts without first checking a consumer's credit history.

How long does it take for a security freeze to be in effect?

Credit bureaus must place the freeze no later than three business days after receiving your written request.

How long does it take to lift a security freeze?

Credit bureaus must lift a freeze no later than three business days after receiving your request.

What will a creditor who requests my file see if it is frozen?

A creditor will see a message or a code indicating that the file is frozen.

Can a creditor get my credit score if my file is frozen?

No. A creditor who requests your file from one of the three credit bureaus will only get a message or a code indicating that the file is frozen.

Can I still get my free annual credit report if my file is frozen?

Yes. To order your free annual credit reports, see our How to Order Your Free Credit Reports. For Experian and TransUnion reports, use the regular procedures for ordering. For Equifax, order by mail using the form included in How to Order Your Free Credit Reports and also provide the PIN issued to you by Equifax when you freeze your file.

Can anyone see my credit file if it is frozen?

When you have a security freeze on your credit file, certain entities still have access to it. Your report can still be released to your existing creditors or to collection agencies acting on their behalf. They can use it to review or collect on your account. Other creditors may also use your information to make offers of credit – unless you opt out of receiving such offers. See below for how to opt out of pre-approved credit offers. Government agencies may have access for collecting child support payments or taxes or for investigating Medical fraud. Government agencies may also have access in response to a court or administrative order, a subpoena, or a search warrant.

Do I have to freeze my file with all three credit bureaus?

Yes. Different credit issuers may use different credit bureaus. If you want to stop your credit file from being viewed, you need to freeze it with Equifax, Experian, and Trans-Union.

Will a freeze lower my credit score?

No.

Can an employer do a background check on me if I have a freeze on my credit file?

No. You would have to lift the freeze to allow a background check or to apply for insurance, just as you would to apply for credit. The process for lifting the freeze is described above.

Does freezing my file mean that I won't receive pre-approved credit offers?

No. You can stop the pre-approved credit offers by calling 888-5OPTOUT (567-8688). Or you can do this online at www.optoutprescreen.com. This will stop most of the offers, the ones that go through the credit bureaus. It's good for five years or you can make it permanent.

Does my spouse's file have to be frozen, too?

Yes, because of community property laws. Both spouses have to freeze their separate credit files, via separate requests, in order to get the benefit. That means the total cost for freezing for consumers under 65 years of age is $10 x 3 credit bureaus x 2 people = $60. For consumers 65 years of age or older, the total cost for freezing is $5 x 3 credit bureaus x 2 people = $30.

What if I lose my PIN?

If you lose the PIN given to you by a credit bureau, send a letter to address on the sample letter attached to this sheet. Explain that you have lost your PIN and would like a new one. Provide your full name, address and Social Security number in the letter. Enclose a photocopy of your driver's license or other government-issued photo ID.

What law requires security freezes?

The California law on security freeze is in the California Consumer Credit Reporting Agencies Act, at California Civil Code §§ 1785.11.2-1785.11.6 and 1785.15.

Sample Freeze Letter to Equifax

[Date]

Equifax

VTSD - Security Freeze

P.O. Box 105788

Atlanta, GA 30348

Dear Equifax:

I would like to place a security freeze on my Equifax credit file.

My full name is:

My current home address is:

My former address was:

My Social Security number is:

My date of birth is:

Please check one:

____ I am under 65 years of age, and I will pay the fee of $10 for placing the freeze

____ I am 65 years of age or older, and I will pay the fee of $5 for placing the freeze

[by check, money order, or credit card]1

OR

____ I am an identity theft victim and a copy of my policy report or DMV investigative report of identity theft is enclosed.

Yours truly,

[Your name and address]

Sample Freeze Letter to Experian

[Date]

Experian Security Freeze

P.O. Box 9554

Allen, TX 75013

Dear Experian:

I would like to place a security freeze on my Experian credit file.

My full name is:

My current home address is:

Below is a list of my addresses for the past two years:

My Social Security number is:

My date of birth is:

As proof of my residence, I am enclosing the following two items:2

Please check one:

___ I am under 65 years of age, and I will pay the fee of $10 for placing the freeze

___ I am 65 years of age or older, and I will pay the fee of $5 for placing the freeze

[by check, money order, or credit card]3

OR

___ I am an identity theft victim and a copy of my police report or

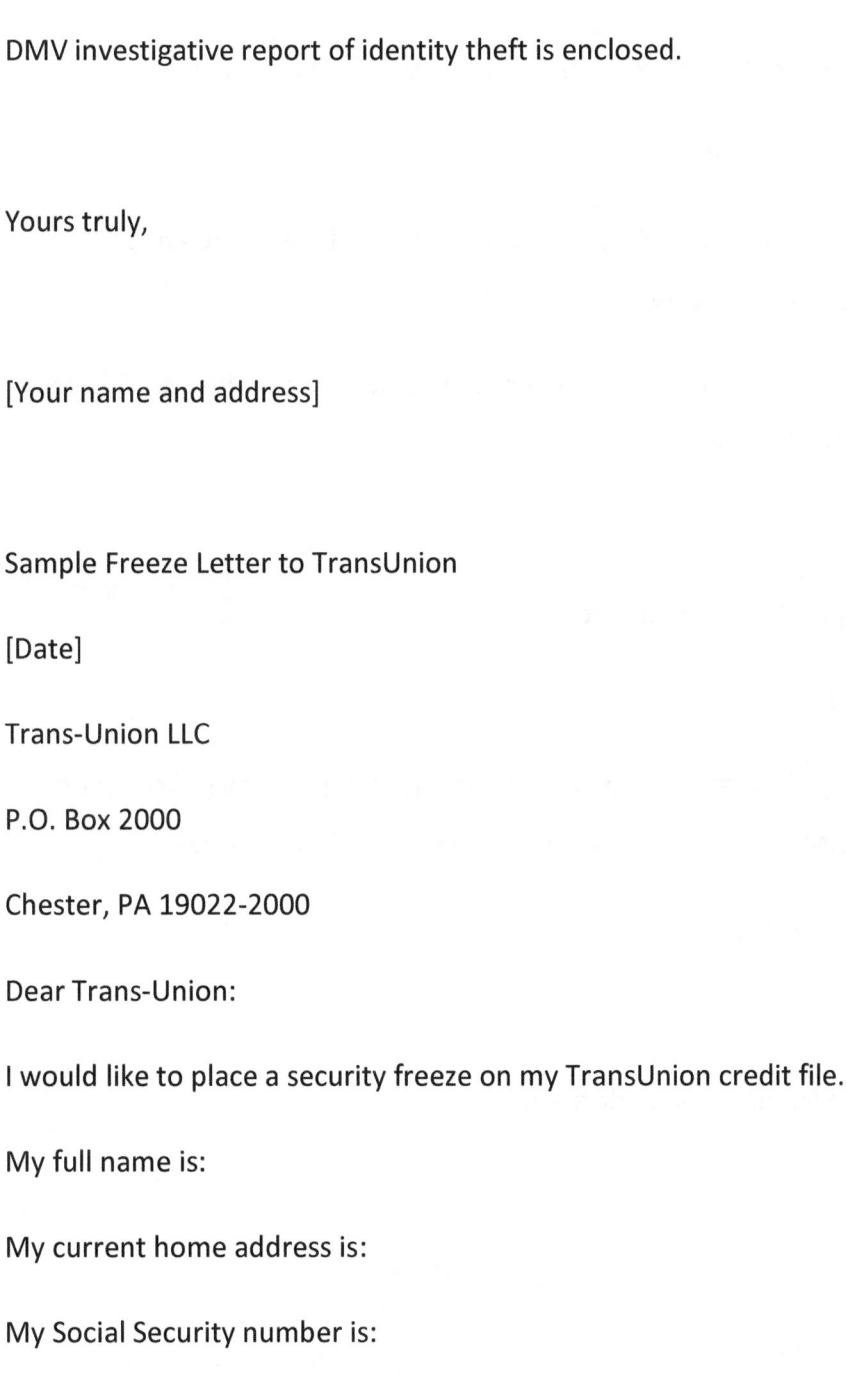

DMV investigative report of identity theft is enclosed.

Yours truly,

[Your name and address]

Sample Freeze Letter to TransUnion

[Date]

Trans-Union LLC

P.O. Box 2000

Chester, PA 19022-2000

Dear Trans-Union:

I would like to place a security freeze on my TransUnion credit file.

My full name is:

My current home address is:

My Social Security number is:

My date of birth is:

As proof of my residence, I am enclosing the following item: 4

Please check one:

____ I am under 65 years of age, and I will pay the fee of $10 for placing the freeze

____ I am 65 years of age or older, and I will pay the fee of $5 for placing the freeze

[by check, money order, or credit card]5

OR

____ I am an identity theft victim and a copy of my police report or DMV investigative report of identity theft is enclosed.

Yours truly,

[Your name and address]

Notes

1. Please include payment for the appropriate fees by check,

money order, or VISA, MasterCard, Discover or American Express. For credit card payment, please include your name as it appears on the card, the card number, and the expiration date.

2 . Enclose a copy of a government issued identification card and a copy of a recent utility bill, bank statement, or insurance statement that displays your name, current mailing address, and the date of issue.

3. For credit card payment, give name of credit card, account number, and expiration date.

4. Enclose a copy of a state issued identification card or driver's license.

5. For credit card payment, give name of credit card, account number, and expiration date.

Addendum I

A Summary of Your Rights

(Under the Fair Credit Reporting Act)

The federal Fair Credit Reporting Act (FCRA) promotes the accuracy, fairness, and privacy of information in the files of consumer reporting agencies. There are many types of consumer reporting agencies, including credit bureaus and specialty agencies (such as agencies that sell information about check writing histories, medical records, and rental history records).

Here is a summary of your major rights under the FCRA.

 For more information, including information about additional rights, go to www.ftc.gov/credit or write to: Consumer Response Center, Room 130-A, Federal Trade Commission, 600 Pennsylvania Ave. N.W., Washington, D.C. 20580.

- You must be told if information in your file has been used against you. Anyone who uses a credit report or another type of consumer report to deny your application for credit, insurance, or employment – or to take another adverse action against you – must tell you, and must give you the name, address, and phone number of the agency that provided the information.

- You have the right to know what is in your file. You may request and obtain all the information about you in the files of a consumer reporting agency (your "file disclosure").
You will be required to provide proper identification, which may include your Social Security number. In many cases, the disclosure will be free. You are entitled to a free file disclosure if:

- a person has taken adverse action against you because of information in your credit report;
- You are the victim of identity theft and place a fraud alert in your file;
- Your file contains inaccurate information as a result of fraud;
- You are on public assistance;
- You are unemployed but expect to apply for employment within 60 days.
- In addition, by September 2005 all consumers will be entitled to one free disclosure every 12 months upon request from each nationwide credit bureau and from nationwide specialty consumer reporting agencies. See www.ftc.gov/credit for additional information.

- You have the right to ask for a credit score. Credit scores are numerical summaries of your credit-worthiness based on information from credit bureaus.

- You may request a credit score from consumer reporting agencies that create scores or distribute scores used in residential real property loans, but you will have to pay for it. In some mortgage transactions, you will receive credit score information for free from the mortgage lender.

- You have the right to dispute incomplete or inaccurate information. If you identify information in your file that is incomplete or inaccurate, and report it to the consumer reporting
agency, the agency must investigate unless your dispute is frivolous. See www.ftc.gov/credit for an explanation of dispute procedures.

- Consumer reporting agencies must correct or delete inaccurate, incomplete, or unverifiable information. Inaccurate, incomplete or unverifiable information must be removed or corrected, usually within 30 days. However, a consumer reporting agency may continue to report information it has verified as accurate.

Addendum II

Summary of the Fair Debt Collection Practices Act

The Fair Debt Collection Practices Act can be used to stop unruly debt collectors.

One of the core elements of successful self credit repair is your ability to deal with all types of collectors. After all, they are the ones who will be making many of the decisions regarding you and your account. Considering this, your success will mostly depend on your ability to handle them. The information in this section is therefore among the most crucial in your quest for exemplary credit.

A summary of the Fair Debt Collection Practices Act (FDCPA)

The term "collectors" generally refers to those who are collecting for themselves (i.e., original creditors), whereas the term "debt collectors" refers to those who are in the business of collecting for third parties, such as collection agencies and lawyers. This distinction is important where laws about how collectors and debt collectors conduct themselves are concerned, because the FDCPA applies only to debt collectors, not inhouse (creditor) collectors.

There are exceptions, however, as certain conduct by creditor collectors can actually bring them under the Fair Debt Collection Practices Act when it would not otherwise apply (see Chapter 14).

A debt collector's contacts with a debtor are known as "duns," regardless of the method of contact. Even debt collectors' dunning letters are governed by the Fair Debt Collection Practices Act, which places tight restrictions on the language they can use. As such, it's extremely important to know your rights before communicating with debt collectors. Such knowledge will provide the basis for the approach you will take and will give you confidence so that you will not allow yourself to be intimidated.

There are two general tests to determine whether a debt collector falls under the FDCPA. One involves the type of collector, and the other involves the type of transaction.

Collectors Covered by the Fair Debt Collection Practices Act

Debt collectors that fall under the Fair Debt Collection Practices Act include the following:

Collection agencies

Attorneys who regularly collect debts

Creditors using a false name

Creditors collecting for another person

Repossession and foreclosure companies (if made unlawfully)

Suppliers or designers of deceptive forms (forms used in collection)

Purchasers of debt after default

Credit counselors (for profit)

Check guarantee services

Third-party collectors collecting for landlords, including attorneys, realty companies, and servicing companies that are collecting rent debts.

Deceptive eviction notices are also covered by the Fair Debt Collection Practices Act. Many state UDAP laws also apply to abusive landlords and their rent collection conduct.

The following types of collectors are generally excluded from the FDCPA:

Creditors who are collecting their own debts

Assignees (i.e., service companies, such as car finance companies, that take on the collection role prior to default on mortgages, student loans, rental agreements, utility bills, medical debts, and other consumer transactions)

Government employees

Business (aka commercial) creditors

Nonprofit credit counselors

Transactions Covered by the Fair Debt Collection Practices Act

Debts that fall under the FDCPA include consumer debts where the transaction was for personal, family, or household purposes, whether or not such obligation has been reduced to judgment. The Act does not apply to commercial debts.

The following are covered by the FDCPA:

- Dishonored checks
- Rent
- Medical bills
- Utility bills
- Insurance bills and claims
- Student loans
- Credit cards
- Condominium fees
- Attorney fees
- Judgments
- Obligations discharged in bankruptcy

- Other personal debts (e.g., parking tickets, auto loans)

Prohibited Practices

The Fair Debt Collection Practices Act defines a debt collector as any person (1) whose principle business is collecting debts, (2) who regularly collects debt owed to a third party, or (3) who uses a false name in the course of debt collection activities or efforts.

The FDCPA prohibits debt collectors from engaging in unfair, deceptive, or abusive practices while collecting debts. The following are the rules under which collection agencies must operate:

- Debt collectors may contact you only between 8 A.M. and 9 P.M.
- Debt collectors may not contact you at work if they know your employer disapproves.
- Debt collectors may not harass, oppress, or abuse you.
- Debt collectors may not lie when collecting debts, such as falsely implying that you have committed a crime.
- Debt collectors must identify themselves to you on the phone.

- Debt collectors must stop contacting you if you ask them to stop in writing (known as a cease communication letter).
- Debt collectors may call your neighbors, but only to determine where you are and only once.
- Debt collectors may not discuss your debts with any third party unless it's your attorney, the creditor's attorney, a credit reporting agency, co debtor, guardian (administrator/executor), or parent (if the debtor is a minor).

In a nutshell, bill collectors from collection agencies cannot harass you by calling late, calling your neighbors repeatedly (or talking to them about your debts), calling your work, or at all! This means that you don't have to be a victim, and you can take action to see that the harassment stops or doesn't occur at all. A cease communication letter is a way to get debt collectors to stop contacting you. This is explained in detail later in this chapter.

Collectors may not make threats

One of the most common illegal actions by debt collectors is to threaten legal action. Debt collectors believe they can get away with such threats because debtors often fear a lawsuit. Few debtors understand that the threat of legal action by debt collectors can actually be spun against them, since any such threat is a violation of the Fair Debt Collection Practices Act. A very broad range of legal threats are in breach, including those that are (1) not intended to be carried out when made, (2) not as imminent as presented, (3) beyond the purview of the debt collector's authority (i.e., those the creditor didn't authorize), or (4) beyond the debt collector's legal authority (e.g., the state forbids lawsuits by collection agencies).

Further, even oblique or disguised threats of a lawsuit on the part of debt collectors are classified as threats under the FDCPA. Examples include claiming that they will agree to settle debts "out of court," saying they "can" sue you, stating that the debt will be referred to a lawyer for debt collection, claiming that they are authorized to proceed with legal action against you, sending a complaint (lawsuit) to a debtor before actually filing it with the court, claiming that "action will be taken" to secure payment in full, listing available creditor remedies (inclusive of legal action), saying "every step will be taken," and marking an envelope with "legal matter enclosed" or the like.

Collector Dunning Letter Requirements

An initial letter from a debt collector must comply with the Fair Debt Collection Practices Act rule requiring that a letter contain the following:

(a) Within five days after the initial communication with a consumer in connection with the collection of any debt, a debt collector shall, unless the following information is contained in the initial communication or the consumer has paid the debt, send the consumer a written notice containing—

(1) the amount of the debt;

(2) the name of the creditor to whom the debt is owed;

(3) a statement that unless the consumer, within thirty days after receipt of the notice, disputes the validity of the debt, or any portion thereof, the debt will be assumed to be valid by the debt collector;

(4) a statement that if the consumer notifies the debt collector in writing within the thirty day period that the debt, or any portion thereof, is disputed, the debt collector will obtain verification of the debt or a copy of a judgment against the consumer and a copy of such verification or judgment will be mailed to the consumer by the debt collector; and

(5) a statement that, upon the consumer's written request within the thirty day period, the debt collector will provide the consumer with the name and address of the original creditor, if different from the current creditor.

(b) If the consumer notifies the debt collector in writing within the thirty day period described in subsection (a) that the debt, or any portion thereof, is disputed, or that the consumer requests the name and address of the original creditor, the debt collector shall cease collection of the debt, or any disputed portion thereof, until the debt collector obtains verification of the debt or any copy of a judgment, or the name and address of the original creditor, and a copy of such verification or judgment, or name and address of the original creditor, is mailed to the consumer by the debt collector.

(c) The failure of a consumer to dispute the validity of a debt under this section may not be construed by any court as an admission of liability by the consumer.

The rules concerning a debt collector's communication are very strict, and even the validation rights notice (paragraph b above) must be placed in such a manner as to avoid confusion to the "least sophisticated consumer." "The law was not made for the protection of experts but for the public—that vast multitude of which includes the ignorant, the unthinking, and the credulous." Not only must a validation notice be present, but it also cannot be obscured by other language, contradict the content of the validation rights, or serve to confuse a debtor. This includes making the font of the validation paragraph smaller than that of the rest of the notice, capitalizing non-validation content, or placing the validation notice on the back of the notice. Demanding payment within 10 days would also serve to confuse or contradict the validation rights by causing a debtor to perceive that he or she actually doesn't have 30 days to dispute a debt under validation. Likewise, threatening lawsuit within 10 days is contradictory.

And there's more. The letter must also contain the name of the creditor, state that the debt is assumed to be valid if it is not disputed, and disclose the exact amount of the debt, not just a principal balance "plus late fees, attorney fees, and interest."

Finagling Subscriber Numbers and Account Identifiers

Bureaus use subscriber numbers to distinguish between furnishers, preventing duplication and reinsertion. Collection agencies know this and will often submit accounts to the bureaus using a new subscriber number for accounts that are outside the seven year limit for credit reporting. This is especially true for sinister agencies that buy old junk debt for pennies. Since collection agencies understand the credit reporting agency's use of queries and filters within their repository, they'll use new or modified account identifiers to get the item to show up on the report when it otherwise wouldn't.

Through this and other illegal methods, the accounts are listed as new on someone's credit file, and then collection attempts resume. Many debtors become frustrated and pay the debts to save their credit, simply because they don't understand that they cannot only get money damages when this happens, but also they can have the collection agencies shut down by notifying the FTC and their state's attorney general.

It's important that consumers dispute any bogus entries with the bureaus, since any affirmation creates huge liability on the part of the furnisher as additional causes of action under the FCRA become available. It can open up the bureau to civil liability as well, so dispute such entries in accordance with Chapter 11.

Violations of Bank Withdrawals

There are two types of bank withdrawals that can be performed by a debt collector. One is a preauthorized draft (demand draft), governed by the Uniform Commercial Code (UCC), and the other is an electronic fund transfer, governed by the Electronic Funds Transfer Act (EFTA). A preauthorized draft is simply a check that a collector prepares and endorses in the account holder's name. This is legal as long as the debtor authorizes it; if not, it is considered fraud, and the collector is liable under the FDCPA and state UDAP or state debt collection laws. And even if the debtor permits a series of preauthorized drafts, the collector must notify the debtor at least three days (and no more than 10 days) before submitting each draft.

The UCC permits the account holder debtor to dispute the bank check as long as the bank is notified "promptly." If the account holder doesn't dispute the initial check, then subsequent checks will be honored, and no remedy is available under the UCC.

In some cases a debtor will authorize a collector to withdraw money directly from a bank account. However, collectors cannot sign a debtor's name for a series of electronic funds transfers (EFTs), as they can with a preauthorized draft. If a collector taps an account without permission, the account holder has 60 days from the statement date (date of a billing statement that includes the transaction) to dispute the transaction and avoid liability for the withdrawal.

If there's no access device (e.g., automated teller machine or debit card) used in the withdrawal, an institution that fails to complete its investigation of a consumer dispute within 10 days and re-credit the account can take 45 days to complete its investigation. This increases to 90 days if an access device was involved. Consumers can also stop payment on EFTs by notifying the financial institution within three business days prior to the scheduled transfer. Banks are liable under the EFTA for failing to perform their duties under the Act.

Regardless of what type of unauthorized withdrawal takes place, a debt collector should also be liable under state UDAPs as well as the FDCPA.

Most banking institutions are also members of the Automated Clearing House (ACH) network and therefore subject to rules that govern electronic transactions, called the National Automated Clearing House Association (NACHA) rules. For more information on this, see the NCLC Consumer Banking and Payments Law (2d ed. 2002 and Supp.).

Telephone Company Violations

For violations of certain provisions by interstate phone companies of the Federal Communications Act (FCA) and Federal Communication Commission (FCC) tariffs (rules and regulations), a consumer can seek a private lawsuit for negligence and breach of telephone contract. This includes a phone company's failure to properly address a complaint made to a telephone company by a consumer against a debt collector. Complaints made to the FCC can be made using its Web site: www.fcc.gov.

In-state breaches are more complicated, depending on state law. Contact the FCC or state Public Utilities Commission (PUC) to find out the enforcer in your state.

NCLC Fair Debt Collection & FDCPA

Addendum III

Budgeting

In order to know where you are financially you must master the art of budgeting.

Small business model

When you need to buy some gum or get a soda, you may sometimes stop at the Stop and Shop store on the nearest corner. This store is part of the cornerstone of the American economy. Of the trillions of dollars earned by businesses in this country a majority of the money is earned by the small businesses just like this Stop and Shop. **All businesses large and small must operate effectively to survive**. The key to each one surviving and thriving is a strong and adequate financial management system. Accounting systems for business are the cornerstone of this financial management system. *Just like a small business your household should utilize a system for tracking your funds and financial situation.* From this point forward, you should consider your household a small business. Let's call it "Your Name Inc."

Like any business your main financial goal will be to maintain a yearly profit, and control your expenses. Also, your business, "Your Name Inc," will want to build assets and provide adequate protection for its employees, and property.

Your first step toward financial stability and strength is a budget. How can someone like a famous singer, or boxer, earn millions of dollars and then end up in bankruptcy? They did not utilize a personal budget. What is the purpose of a budget? *The purpose of a budget is to help your savings grow, to help you in getting all that you need and some of your desires. Most importantly, it is designed to enable you to reach your most cherished future desires.*

What is the first step in the budgeting process? The first step is to get a snapshot of your present financial picture. Without knowing exactly where you are, how can you know where to go? This financial snapshot is called a balance sheet. A balance sheet is used by businesses to assess their financial strengths and weaknesses and you should utilize one to do the same thing. Its simple to design a balance sheet. On the left side list everything you own. This includes your home, car, jewelry, electronics and savings. In the right column make a list of all the things that you owe money on. This includes cars, credit cards, doctor bills and loans. Also include your taxes owed on your property and income. Now subtract what you owe from what you own. And put that remaining number on your sheet in the bottom right corner. You have just created a balance sheet for your small business. This is a snapshot of your present financial picture. Is your net worth, the number that you placed in the right hand corner of your worksheet negative? Is it less than you thought it would be?

This is the first step toward identifying where your money is going. Your balance sheet information can be used in many different ways. To help you get a loan from a bank, or to manage your cash. However, the most important purpose for having a balance sheet is to see how all of your uses of your income are interrelated.

There are three important parts to a balance sheet. These are the ***assets, liabilities and net worth***. Your assets and total liabilities and net-worth should always be the same. This is because your net worth is equal to your assets minus your liabilities. One important aspect to consider and recognize is the type and duration of your liabilities. How much long-term and bad debt do you carry? Long-term debt usually is any debt over two years in duration. This includes loans, auto payments and mortgages. *Believe it or not, your credit card debt should be a short-term debt, because theoretically, it can be paid in full when the monthly statement is received. How many of us can do this?*

When should you complete a balance sheet? Some companies complete a balance once a year, while others do it semi-annually. I feel that it is best to initially complete a balance sheet either monthly or quarterly. This will help you to see your progress as you plan and manage your finances.

The next important tool that you should use in management of your budget is the income statement. I described your balance sheet as a snapshot of your financial situation, a picture of your present financial situation. The income statement is more fluid. Your income statement will show you your actual financial actions and decisions as they occur during the period from when you start the statement to when it ends. It is just like watching a soap opera. Let's say the income statement starts at eleven and ends at noon; you will be able to see everything that happens in between. If you do a monthly income statement, you will be able to see what happened from the first to the thirtieth.

If IBM did not track its expenses and income streams, how long do you think it would last? Not long. *The only entities that can spend more that they earn or bring in and survive for an extended period of time are government entities.* In order to manage your personal finances, you have to know where all of your resources are going. *Furthermore, you must ensure that you do not have more going out than you have coming in.* Management of your cash flow is the number one problem in balancing and controlling your budget.

Could someone have an annual income of fifty thousand dollars and annual debt expenses of forty thousand dollars and be in financial trouble? The answer is yes. What about debt expenses of thirty thousand with the same income? Again the answer is yes. Both of these examples leave a small amount of discretionary income, money not needed for bills, for the person to spend on a monthly basis. If this amount is wasted or exceeded, then all of the budget can be thrown off and this person will have severe financial difficulty.

Here is an example. Mr. Jones has an annual income of $50,000. He will have a monthly income of $4,166. Lets assume his monthly expenses on annual income of $40, 000 would be about $3,333. This would leave only $832 for monthly discretionary expenses such as food, gas, entertainment, education and clothing. This is about $200 a week. The problem in this situation occurs when the Mr. Jones spends over $200 dollars on any given week for his discretionary expenses. He will then be in a cash flow negative situation.

Another way to look at this picture is to recognize just how much money is there for Mr. Jones to save and enjoy after the expenses and needs are met. He has a high monthly income, with very little left over to reach the desires of his heart. On average about fifty dollars a week would be left for savings and future goals.

The income statement, unlike your balance sheet, will only show your sources of incomes and expenses. One thing that you must remember is that your income is a limited resource. This resource, because of its limitations, must be managed, and guarded and used in the most efficient way.

You can only spend a dollar one time.

In my financial planning practice, one of my favorite questions have clients ask themselves when making spending decisions was *"What better other thing can I do with this money."* You see, there are many choices that can be made, and for each choice, there are two certainties that result. The first is that you cannot use that money again. Secondly, the choice you made will have a definite result or reaction.

For example, if you decide to get a new car with a down payment of one thousand dollars, you have made a choice that cannot be changed. That money is spent. Furthermore, the future result or reaction to this choice will be the loss of a portion of your monthly income for several years. Was there a better choice that could have been done with this money? Definitely yes!

For instance, the old car could have been used and the money that would have been a car note saved and invested for a number of years. Then the funds from this account could have been used to purchase a car with a down payment, and the monthly payments made from the same account. You have purchased a new car, but kept your extra cash flow from your income available for optional uses. If you know that your income is a limited resource, and that you must operate like a business, then in order to ensure a profit, you must manage your cost. The money earned as income, must be more than the money spent as expenses. In your budget, you should try to follow several simple but steadfast rules. Firstly, you should control your expenses.

When you first began to work, your level of income was far lower than it is now. However, you were able to live off of it comfortably weren't you? If you sample a room of people, say in a movie theater, many of them will be at totally different income levels, with salaries ranging from twenty to one hundred thousand dollars a year or more. But, most of them would say that they do not have enough money! All of these people are saddled with debt and a small amount of extra cash flow. These facts are true because unless we control our expenses, our expenses will always grow to equal our income, no matter how high it goes. Human nature is that our wants are unlimited, unfortunately, our incomes are limited.

Secondly, you should also begin to save money for the future. Most of us under the pressure of debt assume that there is no way to start saving money. We think, how can we, if we cannot even pay all of the bills? The answer is that you can and you must begin now.

My father always told me to save ten percent of what I make. He would always ask me, "Are you putting some money back?" You must save money for your future and for those rainy days.

"You must save money for the future and rainy days"

Get a glass and a water pitcher, now fill the glass ten times and each time pours the glass of water into the pitcher. Now pour one glass of water back into the glass. Look at how much you still have left in the pitcher. You have more than enough water in the pitcher to quench the thirst of many people. In this way, when you save ten cents of each dollar you earn, you will find you can still do what you need to do as far as bills and other expenses. The benefits of beginning to save are a sense of financial achievement and the knowledge that you have something that is yours. Start now to save ten percent of what you earn. The third rule that you should apply is to increase you income streams. I have spoken about the fact that our income is a limited resource. Also, in the African American community, it is viewed in a negative light to do more than one job. I worked for sixteen years at Local Corporation. At this company, when I began to start my own business or get other sources of income, the other black employees would talk about it in a very negative way. "You must be Jamaican," they would say in very negative tones. What they did not realize, and what I was just beginning to understand was that by learning new skills, and owning a business, or getting another job, no matter how small, expanded my options, and raised the wall of my limitations a little higher.

"Surround yourself with positive people, and don't let other people talk you out of your dreams"

How many businesses succeed and prosper with only one product and one source of income? How risky would this be? What is the stability level of a building's roof with only one pillar holding it up? Many American have found out just how unstable life can be with only one source of income.

Increase your income and knowledge. Give your small business a more stable and less limited income level by having more than one stream of income. Don't let the other negative people or crabs pull you back into the bucket.

When you spend a dollar, what does it really mean? Firstly, as I explained before, you cannot use that dollar anymore. Your money is just like time. Once it is used, it is gone.

Furthermore, by deciding for that specific use of the dollar, you have also chosen against all other possible uses for it. Let me repeat this important fact again.

"When you choose to spend your money on one choice, you are also making a decision against all other possible uses, some of which could be infinitely wiser, for this money."

Another very important consideration that you are not making, and this is one I often stress with my clients to make when formulating their financial plan, is that each dollar is more valuable than you think. In business, there are many considerations of the future value of choices and decisions made. What is the future value of possibly your most important asset, your current income dollars? If you had an extra thousand dollars, say when your taxes came back with a refund, you would have to make a choice about what to do with it. Those choices could be, buy a new riding lawn mower, or use it for a down payment on a new car, or save it in a mutual fund. Each of these choices has a future monetary value. By getting the mower, you have spent the money, with no additional cash flow expenses to look at. Also the money is gone and cannot work for you. If you chose to get the new car, the money would be gone, and an additional cash flow expense would be created in the form of a car note. Thirdly, by putting the money in the mutual fund, you have put the money to work for you, with a possible future value of ten to twenty times what it started out as.

How can you start to lower your expenses so that you can save ten percent of what you earn?

A very good way to do this is by developing a one percent strategy. A one percent strategy is very simple but it is also a very powerful tool for giving you extra cash. There is a point in a company's business cycle when competition is very strong and there is little flexibility in pricing. Also, there are very few opportunities for this business to lower its costs of making the product it sells. When a business faces this type of situation, it must still develop ways to increase its profits. Many businesses will utilize a strategy of cost analysis in all of its areas of operation to cut costs. Each dollar cut from costs goes directly to the bottom line in the form of profits.

The one percent strategy does the same thing for your small business. This is how it works, pull out your income statement and review each expense listed. Figure out one percent of each expense listed. Some of your expenses cannot be reduced, but many of them can and should be reduced by one percent or more. If you spend thirty dollars a week on lunch, and saved 5 percent on this expense, it would only add up to about $1.50 per week or $6 dollars a month. This is only a small part of our budget and is very easy to do. You will find that these small increments of 1 to 5 percent are easy to do. However, the sum is greater that the parts. Once you total up your full savings on a monthly basis, you will be surprised to see a huge amount of money that can be pulled from the expense column with very little change in the way you live. Another way to look at this is to increase quality and efficiency of your business operations. Get three different color pens and make a copy of your income statement. Your first pen will be for cost analysis, use it to take one or more percent from all the expenses you can. Now use another pen to go through all of your expenses with the idea of quality analysis. Do you really need this expense in your life? Does it help the quality of it? Cigarettes could an example of an expensive habit that gets cut by the quality pen. Now use the third pen and go through the statement with the idea of efficiency, what are my waste categories? Where are the places in my budgets where I can be more financially efficient? The choice of which grocery store used can often mean the difference of fifty to one hundred dollars a month in expenses in the food category. Once you have utilized the one percent strategy and the three-pen-method you will have seen several ways to decrease your expenses and increase your monthly cash flow.

Borrowing money can be the downfall of any successful business. When a business carries too much debt, it can too often result of the business going bankrupt. However, all of the most successful businesses borrow money in a way that works positively for them. As you manage your small business, Your Name Inc, you must utilize the same strategies that are used in the business world to make your borrowing work for you. When you make borrowing decisions, it is important to make them with the end result in mind. Too many times we make consumer debt borrowing decisions. We borrow money for cars, jewelry, bills, and even clothing. The only time that most Americans borrow money for positive investments are home purchases and college tuition. By the way, college tuition borrowing is only good if the student does complete college.

Reference

Excerpts from "The Simplified Personal Credit Book"

Addendum IV

Credit Repair Letters

Name/Date
Address
Address
Address
Home and work ph numbers
social security number

I have recently acquired my credit report after carefully reviewing its contents; I have found some **inaccurate information** that the enclosed inserts and credit report detail

Please investigate the accounts listed on the enclosed inserts. Under the provisions of the fair credit reporting act (FCRA) 15 USC section 168i. A period of 30 days shall be " reasonable time" to investigate the accounts in question, unless you notify me immediately otherwise. Failure to verify the above information within the 30 day time period constitutes "non verification" and the accounts in question must be immediately removed from my credit file and credit report according to 15 USC section 1681i(a)

Also 15 USC sections 1681i(d) and 1681j of the Fair Credit Reporting Act require that I receive written notification of the appropriate corrections, an updated credit report, (no charge) and an updated credit report be sent to anyone who received my report within the last six months.

Thank you for your cooperation.

Sincerely,

Enclosures: delete account from my credit report/insert/credit report

Name/Date
Address
Address
Home and work ph numbers
social security number

I (Your Name), request a complimentary copy of my complete credit
report.

My credit report was used in the evaluation of my credit worthiness and
my request for credit was denied. I have enclosed a copy of the denial
letter for your review.

This request is in accordance with the Fair Credit Reporting Act of 1970,
which states the credit agency must provide me with a complimentary
copy of my credit report, based on the denial of credit when requested.
This copy must be provided at no charge.

Please send this copy of my credit report to my address listed above.
Also I have included the following information so that you can provide
the correct copy of credit information.

Date of Birth: _____

Previous Names:

_____

Previous Address:

_____

Spouse Name:

_____

Thank you for your cooperation.

Sincerely,

Sign your name
Print your name

Name/Date
Address
Address
Home and work ph numbers
social security number

I (Your Name), request a complimentary copy of my complete credit report.

My credit report was used in consideration for employment and my credit worthiness. I was denied employment based on the information gathered in the hiring process. I have enclosed a copy of the denial letter for your review.

This request is in accordance with the Fair Credit Reporting Act of 1970, which states the credit agency must provide me with a complimentary copy of my credit report, based on the denial of credit when requested. This copy must be provided at no charge.

Please send this copy of my credit report to my address listed above. Also I have included the following information so that you can provide the correct copy of credit information.

Date of Birth: _____

Previous Names:
_____

Previous Address:
_____

Spouse Name:
_____

Thank you for your cooperation.

Sincerely,

Sign your name

Print your name

Name/Date
Address
Address
Home and work ph numbers
social security number

I (Your Name), request a complimentary copy of my complete credit report.

My credit report was used in consideration for application of rental housing and my credit worthiness. I was denied rental housing based on the information gathered in the background check. I have enclosed a copy of the denial letter for your review.

This request is in accordance with the Fair Credit Reporting Act of 1970, which states the credit agency must provide me with a complimentary copy of my credit report, based on the denial of rental housing when requested. This copy must be provided at no charge.

Please send this copy of my credit report to my address listed above. Also I have included the following information so that you can provide the correct copy of credit information.

Date of Birth: _____

Previous Names:

_____

Previous Address:

_____

Spouse Name:

_____

Thank you for your cooperation.

Sincerely,

Sign your name

Print your name

Your Name
123 Your Street Address
Your City, ST 01234

Credit Bureau
Date:

RE: Dispute Letter of *Date you sent in first or subsequent requests*

Dear Credit Bureau,

This letter is formal notice that you have failed to respond to my dispute letter of *date*. I sent this letter registered mail and have enclosed a copy of the return receipt which you signed on *some date*.

As you are well aware, federal law requires you to respond within 30 days. It has now been over that period since your receipt of my letter. As you are no doubt aware, failure to comply with federal regulations by credit reporting agencies are in serious violation of the Fair Credit Reporting Act and may be investigated by the FTC. Obviously, I am maintaining detailed records of all my correspondence with you.

I am aware that you may have misplaced my letters or have failed to respond to my letter because of an oversight due to the high volume of the requests you receive daily. If this is the case, I'm sure you'll want to handle this matter as soon as possible. For this purpose, I have included a copy of my original request, the dated receipt of your reception of the original letter and a copy of the proof verifying the incorrectness of the credit item you have mistakenly placed on my records.

The following information therefore needs to be verified and deleted from the report as soon as possible:

CREDITOR AGENCY, acct. 123-34567-ABC

Please delete this erroneous item from my credit report as soon as possible.

Sincerely,

your signature

Your Name
SSN# 123-45-6789

Don't forget to provide copies of your original letter and documentation!

Name/Date
Address
Address
Address
Home and work ph numbers
social security number

I (name here), request a complimentary copy of my complete credit report.

This request is in accordance with the state regulations and the Fair Credit Reporting Act of 1970, which states that the credit agency must provide me with a complimentary copy of my credit report once a year, upon request at no charge.

Please send a complete copy of my credit report to my address provided above. To help ensure the correct report is to me, I have provided the following additional information for your use.

Date of Birth: _____

Previous Names:

_____

Previous Address:

_____

Spouse Name: _____

Thank you,

(Sign Name)

(Type Name)

Enclosures: Copy of Driver's License/Copy of another Bill showing your address

Name/Date
Address
Address
Home and work ph numbers
social security number

I have recently acquired my credit report after carefully reviewing its contents, I have found some **outdated inquiry information** that the enclosed inserts and credit report detail

Please investigate the accounts listed on the enclosed inserts. Under the provisions of the fair credit reporting act (FCRA) 15 USC section 168i. A period of 30 days shall be " reasonable time" to investigate the accounts in question, unless you notify me immediately otherwise. Failure to verify the above information within the 30 day time period constitutes "non-verification" and the accounts in question must be immediately removed from my credit file and credit report according to 15 USC section 1681i(a)

Also 15 USC sections 1681i(d) and 1681j of the Fair Credit Reporting Act require that I receive written notification of the appropriate corrections, an updated credit report, (no charge) and an updated credit report be sent to anyone who received my report within the last six months.

Thank you for your cooperation.

Sincerely,

Sign your name

Print your name

Enclosures: delete old inquiry from my credit report/insert/credit report

Name/Date
Address
Address
Address
Home and work ph numbers
social security number

I (Your Name), request a complimentary copy of my complete credit report.

I believe that I have been a victim of credit fraud.

This request is in accordance with the Fair Credit Reporting Act of 1970, which states the credit agency must provide me with a complimentary copy of my credit report, based on being a of credit fraud when requested. This copy must be provided at no charge.

Please send this copy of my credit report to my address listed above. Also I have included the following information so that you can provide the correct copy of credit information.

Date of Birth: _____

Previous Names:

_____

Previous Address:

_____

Spouse Name:

_____

Thank you for your cooperation.

Sincerely,

Sign your name

Print your name

Name/Date
Address
Address
Address
Home and work ph numbers
social security number

I (Your Name), request a complimentary copy of my complete credit report.

I am currently unemployed and will be seeking employment within the next 60 Days.

This request is in accordance with the Fair Credit Reporting Act of 1970, which states the credit agency must provide me with a complimentary copy of my credit report, based on my unemployment seeking employment when requested. This copy must be provided at no charge.

Please send this copy of my credit report to my address listed above. Also I have included the following information so that you can provide the correct copy of credit information.

Date of Birth: _____

Previous Names:

_____

Previous Address:

_____

Spouse Name:

_____

Thank you for your cooperation.

Sincerely,

Sign your name

Print your name

Name/Date
Address
Address
Home and work ph numbers
social security number

I have recently acquired my credit report After carefully reviewing its contents, I have found some **outdated consumer statement information** that the enclosed inserts and credit report detail.

Please investigate the accounts listed on the enclosed inserts. Under the provisions of the fair credit reporting act (FCRA) 15 USC section 168i. A period of 30 days shall be " reasonable time" to investigate the accounts in question, unless you notify me immediately otherwise. Failure to verify the above information within the 30 day time period constitutes "non-verification" and the accounts in question must be immediately removed from my credit file and credit report according to 15 USC section 1681i(a)

Also 15 USC sections 1681i(d) and 1681j of the Fair Credit Reporting Act require that I receive written notification of the appropriate corrections, an updated credit report, (no charge) and an updated credit report be sent to anyone who received my report within the last six months.
Thank you for your cooperation.

Sincerely,

Sign your name

Print your name

Enclosures: delete old consumer statement from my credit report/insert/credit report

About the author

Dewayne Gleeton is an technologist and educator who has worked as a financial advisor for several of the great financial companies such as American Express Financial Advisors, Waddell and Reed Advisors, and John Hancock. He is currently the owner of Advantas Computer, a Media Specialist, and Real-estate Investor. He holds degrees in education and technology from The University of Memphis, (B.S. & M.A.T) and Nova Southeastern University. (E.D. S. Technology)

This book comes with a software download that includes the following:

- **Credit Repair Letters**
  Credit repair letters for different situations that are optimized and written to help you get items removed from your credit.

- **Bankruptcy 101**
  This is a booklet that explains all about bankruptcy. It explains the different types, how they work and much more.

- **Fair Credit Reporting Act**
  We have included a complete copy of the fair credit reporting act so that you can see and use the law.

- **Budget Planning Software**
  Excel based software designed to help you keep and manage your monthly budget. It has all you need to manage, and control your budget so that you can save and invest more.

- **How To Make Extra Money Encyclopedia**
  A great collection of how to books that can show you step by step ways to make extra money. These books cover everything from garage sales to internet sales. This is worth hundreds of dollars in future profits for you!

After purchase send an email to: ceo.advantas@gmail.com for the free download.